MORE POEMS FOR CHILDREN TO ENJOY

AND TEACHERS TOO!

To Lily

BY

ELEANOR MCLEOD

Best wishes
Eleanor McLeod

CheckPoint
Press

More Poems For Children To Enjoy - And Adults Too!
ISBN-13: 978-0-906628-19-2
Published by CheckPoint Press, Ireland

CheckPoint Press
Books With Something to Say..

CHECKPOINT PRESS, DOOAGH, ACHILL ISLAND, CO. MAYO,

REPUBLIC OF IRELAND

TEL: 098 43779

EMAIL: EDITOR@CHECKPOINTPRESS.COM

WEBSITE: WWW.CHECKPOINTPRESS.COM

POEMS FOR CHILDREN TO ENJOY

Eleanor McLeod

Following the enthusiastic reception for her first collection of poems, Eleanor McLeod has now written this second book, full of poems for the Autumn, Spring and Summer terms as well as a lively selection on a variety of subjects, which will certainly be useful for teachers as well as appealing to her young readers who have already enjoyed the rhymes and structures, use of words and images of her imaginative verse.

A review in "SPEECH & DRAMA", the journal of the Society of Teachers of Speech and Drama, of the first book said:

"...a delightful selection of verse...they are immensely accessible, written with simple clarity and with the majority in a rhyming format and with metrical form. They are indeed for children to enjoy ....having some neat insights and observations. (She) has a sharp ear for the way children respond to poetry, consequently they should be read aloud to be fully appreciated, not just at school but in the family."

So, here is the second collection!

CONTENTS

POEMS

FOR THE AUTUMN TERM

REQUIEM FOR SUMMER

So it seems that Summer's dying,
Her last gasps send leaves a-flying,
But the sunshine still is flowing
And her rosy cheeks are glowing
As she faces Autumn's chill.

So it seems that Summer's ending,
Thinly clad her body's trembling,
Warming at the bonfire's bold blaze,
Burning memories of the old days
On a far and smoking hill.

So we sense that Summer's travels
As her flowered gown unravels,
Are now ending with the omen
Of the Winter's icy bowmen
Loosing arrows in the air.

But we know in Summer's slumber
Through the cold days, dark and sombre,
She'll be dreaming of returning
Once the Spring is bright and greening
And the sky is blue and fair.

NEW TERM

Back to school,
In a new class.
Those holidays
Flew by fast!
New timetable,
And teachers too.
When's the next
Holiday due?
Harder work now,
More to learn,
Will it be long
Until half term?
Get confused,
Where am I next?
Going to try to
Do my best.
So many things
To remember.
End of term
Is December!

Eleanor McLeod

AUTUMN ANIMALS

Autumn is a tawny lion
With a shaggy mane,
And roaring as the stormy wind
Shakes out showers of rain.

Autumn is a golden eagle
Spreading its flecked wings.
Fluttering with each leaf that yet
On branches bare still clings.

Autumn is a big brown bear
Shuffling through the beds
Of flowers and shrubs of Summer time,
Ruffling up their heads.

Autumn is a russet fox
Whisking furry tail
With tip of white that soon will bring
Winter's snow and hail.

EXOTIC HARVEST

We all are different in looks and size,
With our colour of hair and shades of eyes,
And the fruit that we bring for Harvest today
Is different, like us, in so many ways.
The curving yellow of a banana
Is like the moon in the skies of Jamaica.
Spiky pineapples that are gold and brown
Wear proudly their sharp Caribbean crown.
While the round, green melons with flesh of red
Reflect the flowers of their tropical bed.
Then oranges, lemons and tangerines
Are like Mediterranean suns it seems.
While the sweetest peaches that blush with pink
Are a little bit like me I like to think!
Rosy apples from the orchards of Kent
Or golden delicious from France are sent.
Then berries are black, and purple the plums.
We bring them together when Harvest comes.

THE HARVEST OF THE SENSES

To watch the ripening wheat grow tall
And carpet all the fields with gold;
To see it waving in the breeze
That foretells Winter's cold;
To gaze upon a flaming sky,
As Summer's eve ends in a blaze
Is to sense the joy of Harvest,
A joy to keep,- amazed.

To smell the tang of woodsmoke now
Softly lingering in the air;
The fresh, sweet scent of new mown hay
As fields are stripped and bare;
To smell the warm deliciousness
Of crisp bread baking, wafting there,
Is to sense the joy of Harvest,
A joy to keep, to share.

To hear the old tractor rumble
Through the whispering corn so high,
The strident call of hovering crow
That whirls and swoops close by;
The children's laughter echoing
Beneath the gentle evening sky,
Is to sense the joy of Harvest,
A joy to keep close by.

To hold the smooth, rosy roundness
Of a crisp apple in your hand;
To scoop up ears of ripened corn
Like many grains of sand;
To feel the warmth of yielding earth
Where the last stook and stalk now stand,
Is to sense the joy of Harvest,
A joy to understand.

To taste the fruits of bush and tree,
That come from near and far away;
The loaves of bread and fresh brown eggs
That nestle on the hay,
This, the final joy of harvest
And the reason why we all say
"Thank you God for your precious gifts
That we enjoy today."

OCTOBER EVENING

A golden evening in October,
The late sun gilding field and tree,
A pink tinged cloud like candyfloss,
One tantalising glimpse of sea.
Where shadows fall they camouflage the path,
A hayrick, Rumpelstiltskin spun
Gleams in the shorn and stubbled fields
Beneath the copper plate of sinking sun.
A flock of birds that sense a warmer place,
Fly in a clear unerring line,
And streaked and striped with scarlet now
The whole of Heaven seems to shine.
And then it's gone – the tints are dulled,
The grey creeps in, the Autumn colour lost
And then the hedges ominously darken
And shudder at the touch of frost.

I'M SURE I SAW A WITCH LAST NIGHT

I'm sure I saw a witch last night
As Halloween drew in.
The sky was clear, the moon was bright,
The wisps of cloud were thin.
Across the lawn I heard a sound,
A rustle in the trees,
A chilling wind blew all around,
Twigs bent like bony knees.
A harsh, dry voice that seemed to moan
Sent shivers through the air.
I sensed that I was not alone,
That someone else was there.
Then, billowing like a deathly shroud,
With gleam of eyes so green,
I saw her fly up high and proud,
Her face set hard and mean.
Across the moon's thin, silver light
She spread her icy grin.
I'm sure I saw a witch last night,
As Halloween set in.

TRICK OR TREAT

Halloween –
What does it mean?
For me it's trick or treat.
In witch's hat
I knock, rat - tat
To claim my bag of sweets.

Halloween –
When ghosts are seen
And little devils too;
And blood beneath
Those vampire teeth
As we scare you – hoo – hoo!

Halloween –
With face of green
And pumpkin lantern bright;
With mask and hood
As spirits should
We frighten you tonight.....BOO!

Halloween –
But then is seen
A strange, dark shape and so
As my heart pounds
I look around
And think I'd better go!

BONFIRE NIGHT

We made an enormous bonfire,
With cardboard and lots of wood,
We built it at the bottom of the garden
Away from the house – as you should.

We stuffed some old clothes for a guy,
I thought he looked rather cool,
And stuck him on top of the fire
Then stood well back – that's the rule.

Dad got the bonfire going,
The flames leapt and roared in the sky,
Then with a howl of horror
Dad looked at the burning guy.

We thought he was going to explode,
Like the rockets, Whizzers and Bouncers,
As he yelled – "Who dressed that man?
He's wearing my best trousers!"

GUY FAWKES

Guy Fawkes tried to blow up
(Some people never grow up)
The King who was due to go up
To the Houses of Parliament.

They caught him with a fuse to
Light the barrels that he'd use to
(I ask you, would you choose to -)
Wreck the Houses of Parliament.

And so we still remember
That strange day in November,
When he nearly made an ember
Of the Houses of Parliament.

We send our rockets sky high
And bonfire flames they fly high,
For the sadly not a wise guy
At the Houses of Parliament.

WHY DO WE HAVE TO HAVE WAR?

Why do we have to have war, Daddy?
Why do we have to have war?
For we're told in school
That loving must rule,
So why do men
Ignore that then?
Why do we have to have war?

Why do men fight each other Daddy?
Why do men fight and kill?
Our teacher says mind
That you're always kind,
But bombs that burst
Can only hurt.
Why do men fight each other?

Why can't we live peacefully Daddy?
Why can't we live peacefully?
Where all men are one
Without tank and gun
No silly wars,
Love evermore.
Why can't we live peacefully?

THE OLD SOLDIER

Standing on the empty
Dunkirk beach,
Fifty years after the war
That took his youth and friends,
The old soldier stands alone.
No words can tell us what he saw,
As he remembers now
What images it sends,
Through this still, peaceful
Afternoon.
Horrors of shock and shell
Ring in his ageing years;
And silently he glances out
Where small boats speed
Across the channel,
As his eyes
Fill with unstoppable tears.

CHRISTMAS TREE

We've just brought home
The Christmas Tree,
It's standing in its pot.
Here come the decorations now,
So let's see what we've got.
First of all come the fairy lights,
All twinkling in a row.
Next some tinsel, silvery white
Sparkling like glistening snow.
Then there are shining golden balls
Reflecting Christmas cheer,
And shimmering glass drops, delicate
As bright and crystal tears.
We've bows and bells and strings of beads,
And on the topmost bough
A lovely, dazzling Christmas star.
Our tree is finished now,
And underneath we'll put the gifts
To open one by one.
How our lovely Christmas tree will smile
To see our joy and fun.

MARY'S LULLABY

Sleep my baby, my little one sleep,
Here in the shelter of my arm,
For all God's angels are hovering to keep
My little son from harm.

Now in the light of a cold winter dawn,
Here on my breast I'll hold you my son,
And close to my heart I will keep you so warm,
My darling little one.

Hear how the angels sing over the earth,
See how the stars so brightly do shine;
They bring the world news
of your great wondrous birth,
But tonight you are mine.

See where the rich kings have come to your manger,
Here at your feet they now humbly fall,
But you who were born as an outcast and stranger
Soon will be king of all.

I have no rich gifts to give you my son,
Sent to this world from Heaven above,
To you just my heart can I offer my little one,
Full of a mother's love.

POEMS

FOR THE SPRING TERM

NEW YEAR RESOLUTION

New year resolution,
What to try?
I could start to keep my bedroom tidy,
Yes – but why?

New year resolution,
Must be good
I ought to save my pocket money
If I could!

New year resolution,
Tricky one….
I'll eat just fruit and salad instead of
Sticky buns.

New year resolution.
Oh, I know!
I'll do my school homework every night.
School…oh no!

SIGNS OF SPRING

A new born lamb,
Curled white
Against its mother
In the field.

A pale faced primrose
Clustered, shy,
Among the joys that
Hedgerows yield.

A fuzzy pussy willow,
Catkin tail,
Nodding in the gusty
April breeze.

A burst of blossoms,
Sunblush pink,
Lone heralds of the
Greening trees.

And yellow daffodils,
Brassy, bold,
Trumpeting the turning
Of the year.

The bloom and bud and burst
Colour, newness,
That says once more that
Spring is here.

I KNOW IT'S SPRING

I know it's Spring
Because I've seen
Nodding snowdrops
In between
The mulch of leaves
That Autumn left,
While in the earth
The bulbs still slept.
I know it's Spring,
Because today
The sun gave me
More time to play,
Before the dark
With sleepy head
Came and put us
Both to bed.
I know it's Spring
Because I heard
The chirping of
A baby bird
In a nest
On the far edge
Of the garden's
Leafy hedge.

SPRING CLEANING

Winter woollie
Shabby pulley,
Don't need you anymore.
In the bag,
No more you'll sag.
Spring cleaning's not a bore!

Pile of comics;
Supersonic
Jet plane with wing that's loose.
Worn out fleeces,
Jigsaw pieces
That aren't of any use.

These shoes that hurt,
A too small skirt
Some books I've read and read.
A broken box,
A pair of socks
From underneath my bed.

Threadbare teddy,
Are you ready
You poor unwanted thing?
Can't be unkind,
I've changed my mind
I'll keep you till next Spring.

SPRINGTIME SNOWMAN

I'm a Springtime snowman,
I shouldn't be here,
There shouldn't be snow
At this time of the year,
But yesterday morning
I saw Jack Frost make
An icing rink
Of the farmyard lake.
And then came the snowflakes
So thick and fast,
Till all the fields
Were covered at last.
And turned to white
Were wall and tree,
And the children came
And they made me.
So here I am
Just standing here
A Springtime snowman
Who shouldn't be there!

SPRING RAIN

Tonight the sky has wept its rainy tears,
And all of Heaven felt sadness now,
Until with morning, how the grey mist clears
And rays of pure sun wipe the sky's damp brow,
Then paint the clouds with pink and violet,
That tremble, mirrored in a puddle's eyes,
And on the wind the scents of Spring are set,
Then hearts are warming as the spirits rise.
The trees that huddled in the damp and gloom
Waiting for Winter's frosty ghost to pass
Begin to smile and bud and leaf and bloom
And Spring puts on her greenest gown at last,
And all this day she'll walk the earth at will
And Heaven will laugh in every blackbird's trill.

Eleanor McLeod

MOTHERS' DAY

I love my Mum.
She's always there to comfort me
When I have scraped an arm or knee;
To read a story after tea.
My cuddly Mum.

I love my Mum.
She makes me brilliant fancy dress,
And helps me with my homework tests;
And when I'm sad she'll always guess.
My clever Mum.

I love my Mum.
You know how handy mothers are,
To take you in her little car
To football or to play guitar.
My useful Mum.

It's Mothers' Day
So I've decided what I'll do –
I'll buy a card and presents too,
And say, "I got these just for you,
I love you Mum."

MARCH

March comes in like a lion,
Roaring along the lane,
Howling round the houses,
So we scamper in again.

Its frosty fangs are sharpest
In icicles hanging low,
Trees and bushes tremble,
As it puffs and pants and blows.

It stalks among the mountains,
With sleety mane and tail,
Whisking up the rivers,
Spitting frosty showers of hail.

Then, its hunger abated,
It lies in sleep so calm
And gently dreaming of Spring
March goes out like a lamb.

EASTER WEEK

There's only a week till Easter,
Hasn't the time gone fast!
It seems like just a moment
Since Christmas hurried past.
But I've finished the chocolate Santa
That my Grandma gave to me
And I do love chocolate eggs —so
I hope there'll be lots for tea!

HOT CROSS BUNS

I don't think a hot cross bun
Looks very cross at all.
It has a sort of smiley face,
And eyes of currants small.
Its cheeks are sweet and sticky,
And it tastes just…well…oh yum!
I'm smiling now because I've eaten
Another hot cross bun!

BE GOOD TO THE EASTER BUNNY

Always be good to the Easter bunny
And he'll be good
To you.

And if you're naughty, it's not funny
Because he knows
That's true.

He's always watching out to see
If you're nice
And so

If you are, then an extra egg
Into his bag
Will go.

And twitching his nose and powder puff tail
He'll hide those eggs
So sweet.

Then you will have to search til you find
Those chocolate
Treats.

PANSY POTTER'S PANCAKES

Peerless are the appealing pancakes
Pansy Potter makes.
Pansy's pleased that such perfection
Is placed upon our plates.
Pansy puts her pretty pancakes
Proudly in the pan.
Pansy, perhaps will possibly
Toss them if she can.
Her performance with her pancakes
Is superb I vow.
Pansy Potter's prodigious pancakes –
Can we eat them now?!

CROWN OF THORNS

And they plaited a crown of thorns
And put it on His head.
The wounds it made were dark and deep,
The blood was pure and red.

And in that crown of agony
Each thorn it had a name;
There was the thorn of poverty,
There was the thorn of pain.

All of the thorns of greed and lust,
Jealousy, hate and more.
The thorns of anger and of spite,
And man with man at war.

The thorns of thoughtlessness and pride
Were twined upon that brow,
And yet those sharp and bitter thorns
Still flourish here and now.

Still we each plait a crown of thorns
And put it on His head.
The wounds they make are dark and deep,
And the shame like blood, is red.

POEMS

FOR THE SUMMER TERM

MAYPOLE

Maypole dancing,
Lively prancing,
Round and round.
Ribbons curling,
Colours twirling,
Tightly wound.
Skirts are swinging,
Bells are ringing,
As we spin.
Music playing,
Dancers swaying
Out and in.
Arms are lifting,
Ribbons twisting
Fast as fast.
Turning, bending,
Now we're ending –
Phew! At last!

BLUEBELLS

The carpet of bluebells covering woodland,
Drifting like smoke on a warm Summer day,
Nodding beneath the newly furled foliage
Is one of the loveliest pleasures of May.

Shadowy haunts of their delicate magic
Ring with the bells in a gentle cascade,
Sweet scents of enchantment rise from the mosses
As they weave their spells in the flowery glade.

Visions of Summer reflected in blueness,
And carefree the pleasure that's promised as well,
So let your heart dance on this magical carpet
Among the delights of beguiling bluebells.

HOMEWORK IN SUMMER

I don't mind some homework in the Winter
When it's dark and I curl up with my book.
And I read or I write what I'm asked to
And I don't give the grass a second look.

But it's not that easy in the Summer
When the evening is as bright as can be
And the park looks awfully inviting,
And the wide open space is calling me.

If I tried to do my sums they'd be wrong,
And I'm grounded when faced with History;
The sun is on the garden and the swing
And that's the place I would much rather be.

So why not keep homework for the Winter,
And give us Summer evenings just to play?
We'd be brighter and fitter and happier.
Why don't teachers listen to what we say?!

ROUNDERS

Now the Summer's come,
It's rounders on the grass,
Red team against the yellow,
Dividing up the class.
Who wants to be the bowler?
Bases, you must stand firm.
I'm in the snaking queue
Waiting my batting turn.
Molly hits it skywards,
And round the square she flies;
But Ruth doesn't hit it,
The sun was in her eyes.
Now I'm stepping forward,
And clutching at my bat,
Must keep the ball in sight,
My teacher told me that.
Here it comes and….oh dear,
Surely there'll be a call?
It was heading downwards –
Oh good, I'm right, "No ball!"
Now she throws once again,
It's a straight and fast one,
Whack! – I think I've hit it
Go on then, quickly, RUN!
First then second bases
Fielders in a flounder,
Three cheers from my team mates,
I have scored a rounder!

SUNFLOWER
(You have to start reading this poem at the bottom!)

and I have won!
my sunflower's biggest
like a wide golden sun
crowned with bright rays
its round halo see
the flower burst
we see
until
still
Higher
grew.
beanstalk
Jack's
Is how
This

Soon it sprouts a leaf or two
Shoots.
Up
Put
To
Starts
It
Then

Keep it watered, feed the roots,
Put it in a sunny spot.
Fill it with earth
In a flower pot,
Tiny seed

HEATWAVE

We're having a real heatwave,
The temperature has soared,
The mark it made in the shade
Was nearing thirty four.

We're having a real heatwave,
Windows are open wide,
But still it's hot and I have got
To do these sums inside.

We're having a real heatwave,
It seems to be the rule,
The blazing sun will always come
When we are still in school.

We're having a real heatwave,
I just can't concentrate.
In a few days it's holidays
And won't that be just great!

MAKING A SAND CASTLE

Choose a spot that firm and flat,
Give the sand a gentle pat,
Dig a moat that's deep and wide,
Put what you've dug out inside
Your bucket, till it's full of sand;
Gently press it with your hand.
Now you turn it upside down,
Tap the top and swivel round.
Then you lift the bucket – and
There's a turret looking grand.
At each corner put one more,
Build a wall to join the four.
Across the moat the drawbridge goes,
They pull it up to keep out foes.
Decorate with shells so bright,
There's your castle – a splendid sight!
None can knock your fortress down
Until the sea will claim its own.

NATURE'S CLASSROOM

Here is the worst day of the week,
        a Monday morning in school,
For after a weekend of sun,
        I'm not really at my best,
My mind is away with the birds
        in skies of blue as a rule,
And all my being yearns to be
        away from this wooden desk.

The lesson that's first will be Maths,
        the numbers roll round my head,
And crowd out the vision of waves
        as they rise and curl and bend.
Each word in French, each German phrase,
        quite simply will leave unsaid
The pleasures I know of that beach
        at the peninsula's end.

In English I try to make sense
        of Milton's "Paradise Lost"
And think of that deep Summer wood
        that is an Eden for me;
If all its wild ingredients
        could be in a potion tossed
This would create more magic than
        a lesson in Chemistry.

For Nature too has a classroom
        that's open to wind and sun.
Its teachers are trees and flowers
        and shells and deep rocky pools,
And there you can learn so much more
        than simply just words and sums
Wouldn't that be the very best
        of the world's most wondrous schools.

BRIEF ENCOUNTER
WITH A BUTTERFLY

Down where the woodland meets the meadow grass,
And sunlight dapples the trees as you pass,
There where the golden buttercup grows,
And the stream goes rippling over your toes,
I saw a butterfly quivering by
Like a pure white rose petal in the sky.
It played hide and seek with the swaying reeds
Touched the wild rose where the bumble bee feeds
Glided like snow on the whispering breeze,
Chasing the sun in and out of the trees.
It brushed past my cheek light and soft and then,
Fluttered into the wood and was gone again.

EVENING LULLABY

Evening brushes softly
On flowers closing eyes,
The breeze to bending branches
Now hums a lullaby.
Shadows put grey nightcaps
On field and mountain far,
In the sky are burning
The candles of the stars.
The clouds will blanket gently
The weary world this night,
And with a quiet prayer,
The sun puts out the light.

Eleanor McLeod

JULY JOY

Summer's term
Nearly done,
Exams are over,
Trophies won,
Oh July joy!

Reports sent,
Reports read!
"Has worked very hard"
Teachers said.
Oh July joy!

No more work,
No more school,
And no more sticking
To the rules.
Oh July Joy!

No rotten homework,
Spoils the day,
No sums or spelling
In the way
Of July joy!

My favourite month,
Sing its praise
There's six whole weeks of
Holidays.
Oh July joy!

PRESSED FLOWER

The small pressed flower behind the glass still sees
The sunny days,
When in the garden, colours called the bees,
And warming rays
Opened the myriad petals to the sky;
And pollen bright
Tempted their fumbling bodies buzzing by
To this rich sight.

The small pressed flower behind the glass still smells
The heavy air.
The roses, phlox, Canterbury bells
All blooming where
The Summer garden in its gorgeous hues
Is painted so
With orange, yellow, purple, pink and blue,
A rich rainbow.

The small pressed flower behind the glass still knows
The Summer's kiss
Where all its face with blushing light still glows;
Ah, how it's missed.
But when the Autumn's cold is blown this way
To frost the grass,
Still caught forever are the Summer days
Behind the glass.

POEMS

ABOUT ME

PROBLEMS
WITH PARENTS

"Eat your breakfast,
Clean your teeth,
And wash behind your ears.
Please keep your knees
As clean as clean,"
That's all a person hears!
Cheeks are shining,
"Look angelic,"
With your hair brushed neatly,
"Sit up straight,
Now stop the scowling,
And try to smile so sweetly."
Your clothes are clean,
And freshly pressed
Your shoes are gleaming too.
"Please don't be rude
Remember manners
That's all we ask of you."
I'll just be patient
And I'll find that
All this brings a prize –
A five pound note
From Auntie Dot,
Well, what a big surprise!

HOMEWORK

I'll do it in a minute,
Because I know I can;
It's just a little riddle
A silly bit of scribble,
That with a tweak and twiddle
And a fiddle in the middle
Will soon work out to plan.

I'll do it in minute,
It's really nothing tough,
Maths is a speciality,
Just some simple numeracy
No need for this anxiety,
I'll soon be sitting pretty
It's easy peasy stuff.

I'll do it in a minute,
I won't take very long.
There are some simple questions,
I'll make a few suggestions,
So don't get indigestion,
This subject is my best one,
I simply won't be wrong.

Right, let's get down to it,
I really mustn't shirk,
This should be just a quickie,
Oh dear, this one is sticky,
It's looking rather tricky,
Mum, I need you – crikey,
This is very hard homework!

A SECRET

Can you keep a secret?
I know I've tried and tried,
But sometimes it's so hard I think
I'm going to burst inside.

Can you keep a secret
Like you've been told to do?
I think this one is about ready
For me to share with you.

You see my secret's this –
I'm going to have a kitten….
There! I'm very glad I told you.
I think I'll be forgiven.

TIMOTHY MY TEDDY

Timothy is my teddy,
He only has one eye,
His nose is wobbling off
And his ears have gone awry.
His arms are stitched back on,
His fur is getting thin,
There's a bit of stuffing
Peeping through his skin.
But I think he's very beautiful,
I wouldn't have another.
I like Timothy my teddy
Better than my brother.

DEAR AGONY AUNT

Dear agony aunt, you know, I'm in such a fix,
My Dad's new wife,
Well I think she's a minx.
She gives me dark looks with her evil eyes
I think she's planning
My swift demise.
What should I do?
Yours,
Snow White.

Give her a mirror that says you are best,
Jealousy and hatred will do the rest.

Dear agony aunt my stepsisters are a pain,
They're ugly too
And they're scrambling my brain.
They want me to be at their beck and call,
Now they won't let me
Go to the ball.
What should I do?
Yours,
Cinderella.

Make sure you've a pumpkin and a few mice,
And welcome old ladies is my advice.

Dear agony aunt, I've got trouble with my Dad,
His attitude
Is now driving me mad.
He won't let me anywhere on my own,
And now I'm sixteen I want to roam.
What should I do?
Yours,
Sleeping Beauty.

Make sure you don't go anywhere creepy
Or very soon you'll feel a bit sleepy.

Dear agony aunt, explain to me please,
Why such a beast
Makes me weak at the knees.
He's quite fat and gross and rather hairy,
I find these feelings
A little bit scary.
What should I do?
Yours,
Beauty.

Don't hold out much hope, you can't change these males,
Beasts only turn to Princes…..in fairy tales.

MY SISTER

I've got a sister,
She's a pain.
She's borrowed my new
Top again.

I've got a sister,
She's a pest.
When she goes out,
That time's best.

I've got a sister,
She's so mean.
Her face is like
A squashed baked bean.

I've got a sister,
She's a bore.
I don't like her
Anymore.

Last week disaster,
She was ill;
And stayed in bed,
Which was brill.

The house was quiet
With no sister.
Do you know what?
I missed her.

TONGUE TWISTERS

I can't say pasghetti
I can't, I've tried and tried,
Sagspetti, spigsatti,
My tongue is really tied.
One last go......
Spaghetti. Hooray!
If you want it faster
Just say pasta!

I can't say tippohatumas
I really wish I could,
Hittomotamus, sippotatumus,
This isn't very good.
One last try......
Hippopotamus. Hooray!
If you want it quick, oh
Just say hippo!

I can't say ritanysaurus
I keep going wrong,
Tyrsanyraumus, sitanysaurus
That word's just too long.
One more try.....
Tyrannosaurus. Hooray!
Yes, as you expect
I'll just say T. Rex.

Isn't English a difficult language?!

THE NEW BABYSITTER

We've got a new babysitter,
Her name is Emilie;
She comes from France
So now is our chance
To practise French – mais oui!

She's got a lovely French accent,
She drives a Peugeot car;
"Be good for me",
says Emilie
And we all think – pourquoi?

And so sometimes we are naughty,
She says, "What 'ave you done?
Snails on my plate
I nearly ate!".
And we reply – pardon.

Our parrot has learnt a lot too
He always tries to say
The things he hears,
So when he swears
It's always – en Francais!

BALLET LESSON

They've sent me to ballet,
Yes honestly – me!
With two left feet
And a graze on my knee.
They've given me pink shoes,
All satin and smooth,
I'd prefer trainers,
But I couldn't choose.
My leotard is mauve,
I look like a plum.
Ballet's not a good idea
And I wish I hadn't come.

GROWNUPS

I cannot understand why grownups always say:
"Of course dear, we will do it on another day",
When what they really mean is, leave it long enough
And I'll forget I asked – I do think that is tough.
And when I want them just to do a special thing,
The answer is: "We'll see". What problems grown ups
bring.
"Well probably", "Perhaps" and "Oh, don't ask me
now",
The answer's always one of those. I ask you how
Can any self respecting child ever get ahead
If everytime he asks them, all that's ever said
Is "Ask your Father", "Just a minute", "Yes, another
time".
When I'm a parent I will answer every child of mine
With, "Yes of course", "we'll do it now", "Certainly,
you bet!".
For that's the kind of answer every child should get!

THE 1ST XV

Thundering down the pitch
Like a herd of wildebeest,
Whizzing down the wing
As if my boots are greased.
I take a lovely pass,
Then tackled to the ground,
Get the ball out quickly,
Support is all around.
They've kicked it into touch,
The lineout ball is ours,
Jump and stretch – we've got it,
With super human powers
And muddy, bruised but strong
We scrum and maul and pass;
Into their twenty two
The line's in sight at last;
The team's like a machine.
The ball is mine – I'll fly
Dodging the opposition,
I ground it – it's a try!

DIVISION REVISION

Later today we've
Division revision,
Oh I wish I was ready and able.
Need to prepare for
Division revision,
By making really sure of my tables.

Division revision,
Division revision,
I must get it into my brain,
Division revision,
Division revision,
I'll go through it just once again.
Division revision,
Division revision
It's driving me really insane.
Division revision,
Division revision,
Division revision's a pain!

Why do they give us
Division revision?
For subtraction and adding aren't too bad.
But when teacher says
Division revision,
Well I know that I'll soon be feeling sad.

Division revision,
Division revision,
Oh what a blot on the day.
Division revision,
Division revision,
No wonder the blue sky's turned grey.
Division revision,
Division revision,
How heavy the thought of it weighs.
Division revision,
Division revision,
Division revision dismay!

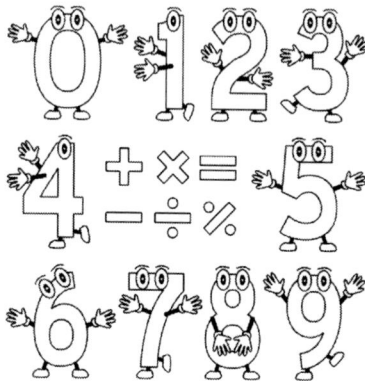

I'M TRYING TO LEARN TO SKIP

I'm trying to learn to skip,
It's terribly, terribly hard,
For I'm always seeming to trip
And falling down – thud – in the yard.

My best friend Jane is teaching me,
And she can skip ever so well.
When I tried to do it with her
I expect you can guess – I fell!

It's all a matter of timing,
As you're jumping over the rope.
I guess I must just keep trying,
As practice makes perfect – I hope!

So here I go swinging it round,
And over my head it goes – flip!
I've done it! It isn't so hard.
Would you like me to teach you to skip!

IF I WAS A PRINCESS

If I was a Princess I would be
Dressed in a silk gown of ivory,
With roses and ribbons in my hair,
And pearls and diamonds everywhere.

If I was a Princess, I would glide
Down palace corridors, long and wide,
And sit on a golden velvet chair,
Whenever I had some time to spare.

And I would say, "Would you kindly bring
My box of rich treasures from the King",
And gleaming inside such gems there'd be,
"Goodness, gracious, are these all for me?"

If I was a Princess my Prince would say,
"Let us marry and come ride away
Together on my milk white horse,
Happy for ever after, of course".

HIDE AND SEEK

Hide and seek is a lot of fun,
The one who's on it counts from one
Right up to twenty – if they can.
It's her turn now. Her name is Ann.

"I'll keep my eyes closed, I won't peep."
Right, she's started, away we creep.
I know a place that's really good,
She'll never find us, she never would.

Oh my goodness, she's got to ten,
We'd better find somewhere quickly then.
I'll hide behind this great big chair,
She'll never find me crouched down there.

Now we're all as quiet as mice,
She'll be coming in a trice.
"Coming! I'll find you, ready or not.
One two three four five I spot.

Out you come, I can see you too,
And you and you and you and you."
Now she's found us, everyone.
See, I told you hide and seek is fun.

DESIGNER CLOTHES
(A teenage wardrobe)

Oh no, you can't expect me to wear that!
It's much too small – no, I'm not getting fat.
It's just that I like them baggy – so please
Can I have a T-shirt that's down to my knees.
It's cool.

Only a wimp would wear those on their feet,
I would be laughed off every street,
They must be the same as my friend next door.
Everyone's got them in Class Four.
They're in.

Oh please, come on, just give me a break,
That jacket it isn't the proper make,
It really makes me look so frumpish
A designer label is just so stylish.
It's hot.

I just can't dress as you want me to,
You really don't understand, do you?
I'm an individual, can't you tell,
And everyone else is like me as well.
We're – different.

A MIXED BAG

After reading my last book, many of you wrote to ask me to write poems about specific things. I hope you have found some of those in this book. The first poem in this section was inspired by your responses.

CAN YOU WRITE ME A POEM?

Can you write me a poem about a rat?
I think I'd like a poem like that.
Rats are furry, with whiskered faces,
Rats have tails like squiggling bootlaces,
With twitching noses and scratchy feet,
My poem about rats is now complete.

Can you write me a poem about a giraffe?
A poem like that would make me laugh.
Giraffes are tall with legs so spindly,
Giraffes chew leaves from the top of a thin tree;
They have necks that would need a very long scarf,
And that's my poem about a giraffe.

Can you write me a poem about a crocodile?
That would be a poem to make me smile.
Crocodiles are crafty, crocodiles are sly,
You can't hear crocodiles as they swim by;
Their teeth are sharp, they sleep in the sun.
My poem about crocodiles is done.

Can you write me a poem about a centipede?
That would be one I'd like to read
The centipede is an agile hunter,
In the garden you might encounter
It shifting on its many pairs of feet.
My poem about a centipede is complete.

What would you like me to write about next?

CARAMEL

I have a small chestnut filly,
I call her Caramel,
I brush her coat until it shines
And comb her tail as well.
And then I get out her saddle,
And put it on her back,
I've polished up her leather reins
And cleaned up all her tack.
Then she and I go out riding
Across the field and lane;
She flicks her long tail with pleasure
And shakes her chocolate mane.
For she and I both together
Are happy as can be.
It's special as we share our ride,
My Caramel and me.

Eleanor McLeod

MRS SPIDER

Mrs Spider slowly spinning
Silky strands of silver thread,
Sparkling, swaying in the sunshine,
But be careful where you tread.
Fearless fly all set to wander,
Unafraid to venture, then
Feet upon the spider's doorstep,
Now he won't fly off again!

Twisting, turning in the tangle,
Trying to be free once more,
Mrs Spider, smiling sweetly,
Spins her silk threads as before.

THE IMPORTANCE OF CATS

Have you once thought how very important
Are cats?
We are mentioned in so many sayings.
There are cat fights
And cat calls,
And copy cats too
And it pours cats and dogs when it's raining.

When you are trying to be crafty you are just like
A cat,
Slyly playing at a cat and mouse game.
So cat burglars
Can cat nap
Or pussy foot round,
But curiosity kills us – what a shame!

What's let out of the bag with a secret?
The cat.
Among the pigeons you put us it seems.
You can either
Have kittens,
Be the cat's whiskers
And then look like the cat that's got the cream!

If a room is much too small what can't you swing?
A cat.
And on a hot tin roof we are leaping.
Who gets your tongue?
Clever cats!
So remember that
When you use us in your purr-fect speaking!

ON THE MENU

In America people eat burgers,
In Italy they have spaghetti,
And in Wales the laverbread
Looks and tastes seaweedy.

In France I'm told they like a snail,
In China they eat chop suey,
In South America you could have
Some crispy nachos and chilli.

In Germany sausage and cabbage you'll get,
In India a spicy curry,
Hungarians make a paprika goulash
And the Japanese raw fish sushi.

In Spain there's a tasty paella,
In Greece moussaka's the dish.
But I like a plate of crunchy chips
Served with a nice bit of fish.

RECYCLING RHYME

You enjoy a bowl of steaming soup,
Thick pea or broth quite thin,
It all goes down into your tum –
But what do you do with the tin?

Packets, bottles, cartons, tins,
Put them in recycling bins.

You munch away at a crackly crisp,
They really make a racket!
Your taste buds tingle with the flavours,
But what do you do with the packet?

Packets, bottles, cartons, tins,
Put them in recycling bins.

A strawberry yoghurt is delicious,
It's what I've set my heart on,
I gobble it down by the spoonful,
But what do I do with the carton?

Packets, bottles, cartons tins,
Put them in recycling bins.

When I'm thirsty I like a coke,
But those who drink a lot'll
Find they are asking the question,
What shall I do with the bottle?

Packets, bottles, cartons tins,
Put them in recycling bins.

A SECOND HAND WORLD

What am I bid for a second hand world,
Tattered round the edges?
It's lost some rainforests here and there,
But we're left with a couple of hedges.
It did have a fancy cap of ice
But it melted just like a dream.
Occasionally it rumbles and blows
And sometimes cracks at the seams.
Some of it's rich and some of it's poor,
It can spew out gas and oil,
Or yield no crops for years and years
In parched and arid soil.
Its inhabitants scatter their waste,
There's a poisoned stream or two;
The air is heavy with industry,
So you see what we've got to do –
We've got to find someone to bid for it,
Despite the holes in its sky,
What is it worth? And do you want it?
Or shall we just leave it to die?
Going….going…..

HANDS
(You could put some actions to this one)

Surrounded by cloth the tailor sits,
Hands neatly sewing stitch after stitch,
Put in the needle, pull through the air,
Fine smart clothes for people to wear.

Inside the church the bellringer stands,
The long, striped bell-rope in his hands.
His two arms are swinging up and down,
Sending the peal out over the town

Now watch the hands of the carpenter,
Busy making cupboard and chair,
Sometimes he hammers so hard and strong,
Sometimes he smoothes the plane along.

There in her office the secretary
Fingers flying quickly over the keys,
At the computer she types away,
Her hands are busy all the day.

Standing in front of the orchestra,
Watch the swift hands of the conductor,
Fast or slow, a smooth automaton,
All the players watch his gliding baton.

Then my mother, holding hands so tight,
That's when you know that it's alright,
A warm hug, a soothing soft caress,
Those are the hands I love the best.

QUESTION AND ANSWER

Sailor, sailor,
Why do you roam
To foreign shores
So far from home?

Maiden, maiden
There's deep in me
The compulsion
Of the sea.

Sailor, sailor,
Where do you go,
As the boat's prow
Goes dipping low?

Maiden maiden,
To countries far,
Guided only
By sun and star

Sailor, sailor,
What do you see,
On your journeys
Over the sea?

Maiden maiden
Spanish gold,
Indian rubies
Of wealth untold.

Sailor, sailor
When will you tire
Of following
Your heart's desire?

Maiden, maiden
I'll never stay,
The sea's command
I must obey.

Sailor, sailor
Are you alone
As you ride high
On busy foam?

Maiden, maiden
With wind and waves
I share my calm
And stormy days.

EVACUEE

I must try to be brave,
But home's so far away,
Oh, this has been so hard,
An awful sort of day.
This gas mask round me neck,
The memory of bombs,
Just hope this war will be
All over soon and gone.
Standing in a row now,
Waiting to be picked,
Really missing mum,
Think I might be sick.
Oh, he seems quite jolly,
I'll smile and hope he'll see,
He's looking over here –
Pick me…oh please pick me.
Still standing in a line,
A label round me neck,
Waiting to be taken.
Just look at her – oh 'eck,

Face as sour as lemons,
I hope she don't choose me;
Phew, she's taken Bobby.
Now, here's the next, let's see.
She is looking kinder,
And younger too I think,
Quite a pretty jumper,
Me Mum's got one in pink.
Oh, she's gone to Jane,
I think I want to cry,
Why do all the nice ones
Just seem to pass me by?
What's that, this one's smiling,
And looking right at me,
And taking home this lonely,
Last evacuee.

A SNAPSHOT OF LIVING

As I sit on a train
With the world whizzing past,
The green banners of trees
All fluttering so fast,
I peep into gardens,
Then through bright windows too,
Just glimpsing so briefly
What other people do.
A football is waiting,
The washing is drying,
On a path in the sun
A black cat is lying.
Here, plates on the table,
There a switched on TV;
Hunched by a computer
A boy seems so busy.
Mum cooks in the kitchen,
Dad is mowing the grass,
With a bucket and sponge
Someone's cleaning the cars.
There's playing and working,
In the sunshine or rain,
A snapshot of living
I see from the train.

FAIRIES

Do you believe in fairies? Are they really true?
Do they live on honey and sip the morning dew?
In their gowns of gossamer, threaded through with light,
Do they dance upon the lawn when the moon is bright?

Do they live in bluebells and foxgloves pink and tall?
Making houses in their cups, delicate and small?
With bumblie bees for postmen, butterflies to ride,
Do you think that I might see them if I peeped inside?

If they wave their silvery wands can they cast a spell?
If they fly into a room, can you always tell?
Do they drop specks of stardust on the window sill?
Will one sit upon my hand if I stay quite still?

Perhaps I'll never see a real fairy queen,
Or even little elves in coats and hats of green.
But when I pass the flowers, I tread with greatest care,
For though I cannot see them, I know that they are there.

Eleanor McLeod

ANOTHER SEASON

If I could create another season,
What would I use,
What would I choose
And for what reason?

I'd choose the mellow gold of Autumn sun,
On burnished trees,
With russet leaves,
Apple, pear and plum.

I'd use white tracery of Winter Frost,
Where it passes
Every grass is
Fragilely embossed.

I'd take the freshest green of early Spring,
The wakening shoot
And stirring root
As new life begins.

I'd let the blue of clearest Summer skies
Reflections make
In stream and lake
Where kingfishers rise.

And I would need no special reason.
As artists do,
I'd paint for you,
Another season,

To capture light and colour here,
Kaleidoscope
Of change and hope
Throughout the year.

ORCHESTRATING THE STORM

The storm's orchestra tunes up.

Now here we have the piquant strings
Of whistling breeze on violins,
Then joining in with muted tones
The stronger wind of deep trombones.
The cymbal clash of thunder comes,
With rumbling rhythms on the drums.
Percussion patters in as rain,
A sharp, insistent, brisk refrain.
Round chimneys trumpets now the gale,
Down alleyways a brassy wail,
And on the flute and clarinet
The swinging gate's shrill note is set.
With baton of the bending bough,
The trees conduct the music now,
A symphony of stormy sound,
This orchestra is all around.

THE MAGIC LESSON

Come along children, bring your pot,
And show me the ingredients that you've got.
Put down that frog James immediately,
And look to the front and listen to me.
Peter, that's not what lizards are for.
Rebecca, catch that rat on the floor!
We won't be doing this lesson today
If you don't pay attention to what I say.
Put in the beetle juice – just a drop,
Oh dear Mary – too much dear – just stop.
Stir in the claws and the whiskers and spit,
And a pinch of pepper, yes Johnny, that's it.
Then chant the words and magic say.
Now Jenny, don't wave your wand round that way.
And "ABRACADABRA!" – Class Three you've
done well,
You've made a successful disappearing spell.
Class Three?!.....

THEATRE GHOSTS
(Dedicated to Swansea Grand Theatre)

Here in the dark auditorium,
The ghosts of the actors roam;
Here you'll find jolly comedians,
Or ever so dramatic tragedians
Who made audiences cheer or moan.

Here on these well trodden boards
Has been many a pantomime;
"Oh no he didn't!", "Oh yes he did!"
"It's right behind you". "Did you boo me then, kid?"
Cheering to the very last line.

Here in these wings lurk the dancers
Whose ballet or tap filled the show;
With high kicks and with twirls,
With point work or with whirls
So gracefully we watched them go.

Under these lights stood the actors,
Declaiming their lines from the Bard,
"To be or not to be…in this play"
"Lend me your ears…and I'll do it this way".
You see, Shakespeare's not really hard!

There in that bright spotlight has stood
The humblest peasant or Queen,
Princesses and dragons,
Mother Courage and her wagon,
So many delights in each scene.

This stage has been peopled with creatures,
From rabbits to sheepdogs or mice,
There's both ends of a horse,
And Jack's cow of course,
And the Ogre who changed in a trice.

In curtain calls, stars and unknowns
And the audience clapped loud and long.
So the next time you're here,
Let's hope you'll all cheer
As the magic of the theatre lives on.

Eleanor McLeod

A QUESTION OF SPACE

What are the stars and where do they go
When the sun shines out in the day?
Are there people living on planets
Whirling in space far away?

Who first saw the Plough and Orion
And who gave the Great Bear its name?
How was the Earth made, millions of years
Before men and animals came?

Is there really a man on the moon?
Is the sun full of flames of fire?
Will we one day find new galaxies
Beyond the stars and higher?

Why can't I see all of the planets
When I look as hard as I can?
Do you think I'll be an astronaut
When I have grown into a man?

THOUGHTS OF A SPACEMAN

Curled in my capsule I await the take-off count,
Thoughts are full of many things, fear and hope and doubt.
My hands and brain alert to set "all systems go"
Heading for the moon now – strange world we do not know.

Families at home with prayers, all eyes heavenwards,
Children proud, excited, wives uttering few words.
Glancing at each other, it's lonely as we wait,
Mission control has suddenly reached 10-9-8

7-6-5-4-3- now our hearts begin to pound,
2 – our fingers tremble turning the dials around,
1 seems the longest second we have ever known…
ZERO – to the moon my friend, to the moon - and home!

THE MOON'S VOYAGE

Gently the moon the other night
Went gliding, gliding by;
A curved sail on a starry flight
Across the seas of sky.

Gently the moon the other day
Kept gliding, gliding on
Until it furled its silver sail
When all the stars had gone.

LULLABY

Night and silence close the day,
Now the deep
Drifts of sleep
Sandman sprinkles on his way.

Close your eyes my little one,
Moon so bright
Spills her light
Softly now the dark has come.

God's own angels watch your bed,
Till through dreams,
Morning beams,
Safely slumber, sleepy head.